00001807704371

Senses in My World

Touching

by Martha E. H. Rustad

Bullfrog
Books

Ideas for Parents and Teachers

Bullfrog Books let children practice reading informational text at the earliest reading levels. Repetition, familiar words, and photo labels support early readers.

Before Reading

- Ask the child to think about senses. Ask: How do you touch and feel?

- Look at the picture glossary together. Read and discuss the words.

Read the Book

- "Walk" through the book and look at the photos. Let the child ask questions. Point out the photo labels.

- Read the book to the child, or have him or her read independently.

After Reading

- Prompt the child to think more. Ask: What things do you feel around you? How does your sense of touch help you learn?

Bullfrog Books are published by Jump!
5357 Penn Avenue South
Minneapolis, MN 55419
www.jumplibrary.com

Copyright © 2015 Jump! International copyright reserved in all countries. No part of this book may be reproduced in any form without written permission from the publisher.

Rustad, Martha E. H. (Martha Elizabeth Hillman), 1975- author.
  Touching / by Martha E.H. Rustad.
    pages cm. — (Senses in my world)
  Summary: "This photo-illustrated book for young readers describes how the brain senses touch and what we learn about our surroundings through our sense of touch" — Provided by publisher.
  Audience: Ages 5-8.
  Audience: K to grade 3.
  ISBN 978-1-62031-119-6 (hardcover) —
  ISBN 978-1-62496-186-1 (ebook) —
  ISBN 978-1-62031-153-0 (paperback)
  1. Touch — Juvenile literature. 2. Senses and sensation — Juvenile literature. I. Title.
  QP451.R87 2015
  612.8'8—dc23
                                    2014000777

Series Editor: Rebecca Glaser
Series Designer: Ellen Huber
Book Designer: Anna Peterson
Photo Researcher: Kurtis Kinneman

Photo Credits: Corbis/Image Source, 6–7; Corbis/Tomas Rodriguez, 8–9; Getty Images/MIXA Next, 10–11; iStock/RobMattingley, cover; Shutterstock/Andrey Arkusha, 16; Shutterstock/CLIPAREA I Custom media, 7 (inset), 23tl; Shutterstock/gdvcom, 1; Shutterstock/HandmadePictures, 12; Shutterstock/Kzenon, 14–15, 23tr; Shutterstock/lapas77, 17; Shutterstock/Mark Hayes, 8 (inset), 23bl; Shutterstock/MaszaS, 3; Shutterstock/snapgalleria, 22; Shutterstock/Stanislav Komogorov, 13; Shutterstock/Syda Productions, 4, 5, 24; Shutterstock/Zurijeta, 20–21, 23br; SuperStock/Blue Jean Images, 18–19

Printed in the United States of America at Corporate Graphics, in North Mankato, Minnesota.
6-2014
10 9 8 7 6 5 4 3 2 1

Table of Contents

How Do We Touch?

Touch is one of our senses.

How does it work?

The skin feels what we touch.

Nerves are under the skin.

They send a message.

The brain understands
it as touch.

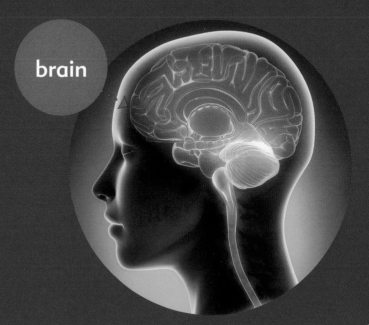

brain

What do we feel?

Roxy feels a cup of cocoa.

It is hot.

She waits for it to cool.

Lee feels the table.

It is sticky.

He needs to wipe it.

Sal bumps a cactus.
Ouch!

cactus

12

It is sharp.

He stays away from it.

Dan walks on the path.

It feels icy.

He needs to slow down.

Jo feels the wind.

It is cold.

She puts on a hat.

Evan's mom touches
his hand.

He knows she loves him.

What do you touch?

What does it tell you?

Parts of the Skin

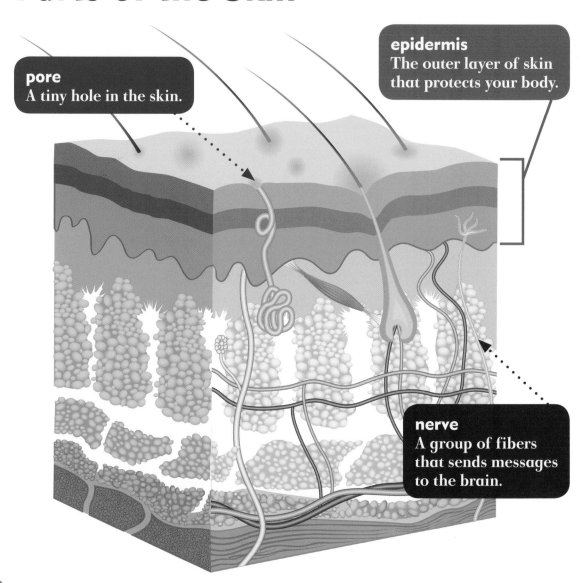

pore
A tiny hole in the skin.

epidermis
The outer layer of skin that protects your body.

nerve
A group of fibers that sends messages to the brain.

Picture Glossary

brain
A body part in your head that helps you think and understand.

icy
Coated with frozen water.

cocoa
A hot drink made from chocolate.

sense
A way of knowing about things around you; you have five senses.

Index

To Learn More

Learning more is as easy as 1, 2, 3.

1) Go to www.factsurfer.com

2) Enter "touching" into the search box.

3) Click the "Surf" button to see a list of websites.

With factsurfer.com, finding more information is just a click away.